AF471679

Acknowledgments

Varquis would like to thank the following

First and foremost I would like to thank God for giving me life and giving me the gift of writing, you are the source of my creativity and my life and this truly would not be possible without you.
My grandmother (Mary Alice Johnson) my heart the reason I am who I am, you know me best no matter how hard I try words really cannot express how I feel about you, you are a queen an angelic woman, you personified what love is and I want to thank you for that because you showed me what that is I miss you a lot grandma and thanks for everything and you are a major reason for this book. I dedicate this book to you (I love you)---my mom I appreciate you being there for me, I'm going to be able to take care of you 1 day, you mean more to me than you will ever know and little do you know but we are a lot alike.
You are my heart (I love you)---my Popz I want to thank you for the constant and relevant talks and for keeping me sharp you don't think so but I listen and don't worry I'm going to carry out the family name with class. Mom & Popz the both of you were a big inspiration for this book and I love you both.---my brother dris remember you are a king and to always keep it real with yourself 1life 1love---my sister Dee, Aisha, Tonia you are queens just remember that and carry yourselves as such and demand respect I love ya'll---the entire Johnson, smith, Jones family,1love to all of my aunts, uncles & cousins---I would like to thank Mr. Elmon Prier, I would like you to know that you helped inspire this book, much love thank you--- Shoutout to my partner Damien McPherson thanks for all of your contributions and great advice bro let's make history Soulsike -- Darius Prier I would like to thank you for your support and encouragement.---shoutout to my cousin KR, we are building from the ground up in every aspect of life, lets continue to be the kingz that we were born to be no one understands us but our time is coming,---I also want to thank Darryl for the pictures god bless---I would like to thank the city from which I come from the ghetto inspired me to want to get out and be successful also the genuine friends and those who supported Varquis you know who you are and thanks for purchasing this book

1 life 1 love,
Varquis

Introduction ("Breathe In")

Breath is a collection of thoughts, experiences, emotions trials tribulations and views since the beginning of my life an over view if you will. I began writing this book in 1999 and completed it in 2003. I want you to take each poem and apply it to your life as it relates and hopefully you will obtain something from it to help you 'breathe' a little easier. To breathe is to inhale and exhale air, to be alive and to live

Take a deep breath relax your mind clear your mind to breathe is to inhale life
We must face it; face it we all come to be at war with ourselves
Striving for perfection, surviving in the meantime the clock ticks, they say it doesn't stop and it doesn't wait on no one
I breathe life into these words as they exist in all of us
So take a deep breath and just breathe

"The Jewel"

Since I can remember I always wanted to know why I was born and why I even existed, what is my purpose in life, it came to me 1 day, I have to find myself, discover who I am and know and understand who I am,
So the jewel is to find yourself and your purpose in life and know and understand who you are the positive the negative the good the bad, be a leader and never a follower and last but not least stay true to yourself

"5 Years Old"

I fell in love with this at 5 years old
I could see myself there, there was my idols, mocking every move and jester then making it my own, on into the next day after day, how could I described the passion that I have for my 1st love she never leaves me she never left me but I left her briefly and she was still with me still there for me I was committed to her and she was committed to me in high school we were real close spending everyday together always together people are getting use to seeing us together now we complemented each other very well we speak the same language and we became successful together we were inseparable I was dedicated when I left high school I followed her from Ohio all the way to Missouri to try to continue the success that we had in high school and once I got there someone came in between us for a while it knocked me off my feet once again it rained on my parade with no remorse and for years to come it would continue to rain when I left her in Missouri she followed me back to Ohio I knew it would be a change and it was not the same we were close but not as close as we once were years passed and we are not together ,I watch her from a distance on the television now it makes me want to be with her like before, we hang out every now and then and she & I were great together so I was told and when I see her and we are together I still get the same feeling I got when I was 5 years old....I love basketball

“Directions”

North south east west which way do I go?
Which way do I turn?
So much to do and very little time and sometimes I don’t have enough of that this 10 letter word takes me from 1 to the next just like that and right back to where I stared I need to get away from there I don’t care how I do it I need to be like Nike and well you know ...I’m looking out a window of opportunity but with a lot on my mind I am from a ghetto community I call myself a navigator and right now I don’t even know which way to go, but I do know that it’s all about me and where I want to be, you can try and come see what I’m really about but you’ll end up with no luck, I got no time to fool around with ..Women with immature minds and.... N...as who don’t want nothing out of life like the world in their hands type of shit, that type is non-productive but this star will make it with or without ya’ll and stand on my own 2 like I always have and always do because god wakes me up in the morning so I have 2, because the direction I’m going too will lead me to the gold with the pot of it...directions.... The 1’s I take are from the most high and the direction I take is on a path of perfecting...myself.... Directions

"Deep Sleep"

I arrest sound and put it in my captivity, reality my physical athletic, possessing championships with handwritten skills too, together get it better late than never, but some dream big and think small I battle with 4 walls just to reach ya'll not to preach ya'll, she asked me to open up, I broke it down explained it so she'd understand it don't plan on it because shit happens. People change, it still rains then begins again like the sunrise on Sundays, for now on I conceal my treasure box you want it come and find it. But its hard too because I set up obstacles just like god do, I sleep deeply waiting for the wind to blow in my direction so I can go on a ride to perfection it ends at a period of existence, I return to my sacred persona where I'm the only 1 with a key and a spare, I sleep deeply I make it hard to peep me it's hard to read me but very well I can read, I don't really need to study for your class I passed yours you might find me chillin on the ocean floor speaking to the mast-or, I look snake eyes in the face and box with hate, arm-wrestle with stress and test myself, right now its best I stay to it I utilize tools mechanics don't use to build upon the ghetto blues then the smooth tunes of a jazz melody eases the pain steadily so I can go on with my life....I sleep deeply

"I Stimulate Her Mind without Asking"

You can feel my pulse in your veins
Am I vain when I say I know I could have you and I know how to treat you when I speak the pulse thumps harder and the idea of us together is in your blood stream and it rushes to your brain striking a nerve making you get the nerve to ask me if we could be an item. I stimulate her mind without asking I don't need her permission the way I speak creates curiosity and she is wondering if who I present myself to be is truly who I am either way she is intrigued by my aura causing her to want to stay in my arena forever in my dimension of seduction, when you breathe I hold your breath captive and when I release it you feel me again, you force me to continue my truth is now in you and the truth is you can feel my pulse in your veins

“In Luv with My Past”

I find myself falling in luv with my past I dwell in it
I was much happier then a sweet blend of anger,
confusion a few smiles everything one could imagine, I
find myself seeing me daydreaming about my past my
past...I see my future but I can’t see the future no future
with a past, so pleasant yet so horrible it kills me to luv
my past don’t ask to painful, to vivid your mind would
not understand nor understood even after I took the
time to explain my past much more than just emotional
pain much more than that, I feel it in my guts you’re not
like me so u feel nothing at all my past is pain so feel this
it’s hard for you too only if you walked in my shoes but
you ain’t me

"I am Not Perfect Not By A Long Shot"

I am not perfect not by a long shot
My words are all that I've got
Parts of my life are private stored away forever
My ways are often misunderstood
I stood alone most of the time
And I will die that way for sure
I stand by my beliefs until I am no more
Only to disappear into the sun and the rain will fall next to me while in my grave
As I am 1 with the earth I was told it is a gift & a curse
I'm dying to live but ready to go but ready to stay
I have so much to live for, stand still
Seems like my wishes are coming true
I'm not sure if I really want that
And I am not perfect not by a long shot understand that

"I Ain't Living"

I ain't livin, the hands of life come and choke the life out
of me often it's not often I get to breathe
My needs never get met they never meet seems like they
never will seems like the devil's will is to stop me from
experiencing success, I ain't livin it's a price for success
stress calls my name everyday never missing a call never
missing a day
It hopes that I fall all my life I've crawled I'm ready to
run....away...carry myself away because I ain't livin, love
is missing in fact love never loved me back not even
when I showed it my mother's mother passed and my
heart exploded
It's been years and I'm still not over...it...the hands of
poverty grab me and my people and that ain't livin
I feel dead already absolutely...yes... I want to live
I want kids, I want a house, I want a yard, I want things,
I want my children to have swings I want my daughter to
be a queen I want my son to be a king for now it's just a
dream because I ain't livin

"Forgive Me I'm A Dreamer"

I wake up from yet another 1 of my big dreams & aspirations
It's exhausting as I continue to dream I can't help it
I daydream and say things to myself that make me believe in myself so I can believe that my dreams can happen
Forgive me I know they seem outlandish but I'm a dreamer
I have a dream fetish ya'll and I'm chasing my dreams until I run out of breath until my death, my dreams are fragments of the truth fragments of imagination, I am truly a dream chaser with a promising destination, I dream of things I can't touch, I can hardly see the dream the light at the end of the tunnel is dim I wipe my eyes to get a clear view, I have a vision and so I ask those dreams of success are too far fetch says who?

"Mama Gotta Life Too"

Mama gotta life too, those are the words coming from those who give birth to us, mama like to party and often leaves the children alone at home...unattended to fend for themselves
U see mama may have lost out on some of her childhood and she was a baby when she had her babies, not being able to enjoy her life she had responsibly but mama gotta life too and she's trying to get it back, so she goes out to have herself a good time and at times forgets that she has children, in the minds and spirits of those children they scream mama we need you, well mama gotta life too, and the father isn't there so we have no one to turn too, and mama out doing her thing, therefore the children become independent with very little guidance and no supervision, so I pray for the lord to guide us, mama we need you
We need you around to feed us more than just food we need to be fed jewels, we need to be fed life, we need quality time, we need to bond, I understand but all she tells us is mama gotta life too

“I Exist In Pain”

I exist in pain I been through it felt it seen it
I feel pain that pierces through my flesh like a thousand thorns my pride has been torn a thousand times
I come from pain and anguish and stressful days it doesn’t pay to have good intentions those things are never mentioned they are lost in this world of deception the perception the world had about me is that everything is ok, that is far from the truth I am seeking it but I am far from the truth
Maybe I am close because they say it’s a little truth in everything even me, I expand myself evenly seemingly spreading myself to thin, not at all but my hands are in everything trying to get a hold on everything and making sure nothing gets a hold of me, the world holds me captive though, trap in a world wind of life’s issues, I lay my problems flat on the board to iron them out and do away with the wrinkles but you know they like to come back I fight them off with a large amount of sips from my bottle of liquid crack but I wake up to the same pain that I exist in....pain

"The City Limits"

Born and raised within the city limits
The city limits the city limits
The city limits us; the city limits us from a lot of things
The city limits us from the dreams we have
The city limits us from a decent education
The city limits us from being able to see the world
The city limits us from a decent living
It limits us from seeing beyond those ghetto blocks we
are confined to mind you... I am young black & gifted
The city limits us from seeing the big picture
From knowing it's more out there, sometimes the city
limits us from growing the city sometimes limits us from
becoming something, contributing to something greater
than ourselves
Keeping our minds closed with no direction of where we
want to go, I come from a city where some are content
with living mediocre, the city limits boys from becoming
men
But I won't let the city limit me

"A Story from the Ghetto" (A True Story)

He grew up foul, ghetto with ambitions and goals, Had crazy flow, He sold a little
He held guns before Held his position down in front of corner stores, ready to go to war, He kind of quiet mistaken for soft, at any moment he could go off, kept the ladies clothes off, just recently became a doe chaser his middle name should be paper known to shallow alcohol till he about to fall street smart though but slipped up and got bagged a few times bagged a few dimes watched out for snitch niggas and fake bitches he keep his eyes on his riches, pop wasn't there when he was younger part of the hunger, no fear, he plans on eating competing and staying competitive the music is his medicine beats the I.V he shoot up every week, overdose he grab a bottle of something and toast to his self he think like he only got 1 life to live and he'll be damned if u think about taking his, he show signs of class don't get it fucked up he still gutter part of the town where he's from is the slum nigga its dark but the brightest light still shines bigger, understand me

Word on the street that man nice with his and he run wild with a bunch of shiesty kids trying to avoid doing any type of bid but that dirty money got him up to no good my place was clean but it was still in the hood my heart still in the hood
Niggas get locked up for good I kind of think like Suge test my manhood I wish you would I seen coke sniffed right in front of my face crack fiends in and out the place was young so I really didn't recognize their face, I feel ya, seen them on the street damn they looked familiar Douglas park the narcs creep after dark on the corner of the block at the party I witnessed a nigga get shot my city if filled up with crooked cops waiting for niggas to make the drop so they can sit back and put us on lock it's my..life or yours keep stepping I'm soon to become a holder of a concealed weapon I call my gun the rubber its used for protection who is the next in...line to get popped by a cop who says he's just doing his job..Bullshit! And you get the middle finger we will have the glory...from the ghetto this is a true story

“Black Rose”

I started from nothing strong and beautiful
I’m praying for something/worth living for
My heart is pumping passion for the love of this life and family
I’m asking God to save me give me your blessing
Lord show me the light and give me direction
I know he in disguise the devil is testing
And I’m on my grind no time for resting
I’m true to myself my time’s invested wisely
Can’t wait for my niggas behind me was told to be aggressive
Niggas and chickens all in my mix I use discretion
Was born into sin but I strive for perfection it’s strange it’s easy
My people get caught up in the game
Don’t read books but I pick up on the latest slang
Get bagged and go to jail be back no thang
My niggas from my hood grow up and feel pain
It’s no thang cuz we use to it wanna gain material things the chains and the diamond rings, but we struggle it ain’t all fine and dandy
I cope wit it in the cut sipping on brandy E&J
Till the problems fade away but they don’t

Now I’m drunk on the low laughing ain’t nothing funny serious as asthma
When it come to getting money, despite all my contradictions niggas they still listen hustlers on the corner this life will cause friction I won’t quite on my dream
That’s what they call persistence keep snakes at a distance they try to get to close
I can hear them hissing they got excuses it useless man we come from poverty
Most of us are talented we become a commodity but some of us give in to the drug life probably the city where I’m from tries to trap me its politics but I try to prosper ignore the gossip the cops sit and watch us but nothing gone stop us
The dirt that I did still lingers on my conscience

If it was up to me I would free all my people in the ghetto sit them in a mansion
Show them how to live pass the wealth to their kids dig I search for a life more suitable for me I’m a black rose strong & beautiful to my women you’re the queens to the throne my niggas we’re the kings lets live till we’re gone

"Angelic Woman"

Mary Johnson I still hear ya voice like constant
Stitched in my brain since the day you left me I cried for months asking God why he took you that was too early I need you, you use to feed me food & jewels
You taught me about Jesus now you up there with Jesus why you leave us
I guess God has his reasons but I don't understand them it's your oldest grandson
You gone but I'm still trying to get you that mansion that I promised I promise
I'm going to take care of the family for you and put them on my shoulders
Your words were true and your actions spoke for you responsibility I take as you did raising me into the man that I am today, you instilled qualities I could have only learned from you I learned a lot from you I miss you and need to talk to you
More than ever I need my grandmother with me I keep her close to me
I spirit I still can hear you your presence is felt in the form of your children and grandchildren continuing to build the legacy you started you had love that touched everyone you came across and that rubbed off on me through you I seen how a woman should be a true angel on earth I don't know anyone else more genuine and more true than the word itself there will never be another like you
A black rose describes you best strength & beauty with a heart of gold a woman of royalty not many are like...she made sacrifices and went above and beyond her duty
God must be proud as I am proud to be her grandson I stand here today because God blow breath in my lungs and a king was raised by an angelic woman that I love ...forever

“Family”

Family we don’t always get along but we love each other anyway
I can talk about u but no one else can
Sometimes we fight each other but the love is unconditional
No matter what we are here for each other
If I got it you got it and if I don’t have it I’m going to get it for you
We are forever connected by the blood in our veins
Therefore I feel your pain when you hurt I hurt and when you shed tears
I shed tears if you fight we all are fighting
If I eat we all are eating
If I make it we all make it
No matter what we are here our children will continue the tradition
Generation after generation and they will carry out the name proudly as we do
To be continued...

"Write Before Your Eyes"

Boom!... Life is right in front of you
God and the devil they both got an eye on you
I spy on myself to check what I'm doing
I wake up to it somewhat trap in this bubble
Where it's oceans of water and land that I haven't seen yet
Only on maps not too much dap is given in a huddle
Where they shoot craps at competing everyday to get doe stacked I
Suppose that's how they pass time but peace of mind can be blind to the
Naked eye sometimes and poverty lives in my eyes accompanied by lies
And compliments of the 2nd name in the 2nd line
Gun shots fired from the 9 duck down the bullets ricochet off the town
Just because somebody was looking at him crazy
Problems stand in front of me like my face in the mirror
Fiening to see the world clearer but all I see are single parents with 3 or 4 kids
1 getting ready to do his 1st bid with a kid of his own who screams I'm grown
But look where they live though gotta grow up fast because life will pass right by you like cars in the dark when you walk; I'm in the ghetto where it's cracked glass
In the street burn down abandoned buildings and the birds see the same things I see my anger speaks to me and sometimes I listen I see the world in many angles which reflect back to me but its write before your eyes...look!

"Purpose"

I hold back the water glands in my eyes
On purpose
Not allowing them to reach the surface of my face
On purpose
I was born for a purpose
I was born for a purpose
Pardon me but I drink with a purpose
I read and eat with a purpose
They say God has a purpose what is his purpose for me
Who knows who knew he would have turned out like
this?
Still searching for his purpose
Not knowing the reason for his existence
Looking in different directions to find the purpose
And ask yourself what is my purpose

"God Body"

My speeches reaches as far as the end of the oceans
It's God sent so I sent him back devotion
I seek the truth and for a closer bond with you
I ask for your blessing the shape of this man comes from life's lessons
While I'm working on myself you are still working on me
I have a lot to work on I'm still polishing my edges
I get edgy trying to control my devilish temper
Temptation grabs a hold of me fiercely
So intense like this ever since I knew what temptation was
I'm wrong when I pray every blue moon
Hoping you forgive that I am a sinner in certain aspects
I confessed that I have sinned but I want you within
The 4 chambers of my blood organ
I've heard of your word and I look into it to understand it and to see what your speak of
You have a plan for me
A purpose for me
And to the best of my ability I'm going to live out your will for me
I love you God and in Jesus name we pray amen...

“I Rise Like the Sunshine”

I rise like the sunshine just like the horizon
I was ahead of my time in my prime black men are prime suspects
The subject of many discussions discussed with society we still rise
To your surprise my pride gets in the way a lot of times
It’s too strong it’s hard to get out of my own way
The powers that be make it hard for us to make a way
From the rims of life I want to break away, but I rise like the sun every morning
It rains on my parade daily the forecast shows that it’s certainly going to rain again but I rise like the horizon and I rise above racism which still exists by the way...hatred stereotypes etc... in a world of politics we fight for our slice of the
American dream which is really not created for us but we rise like the sunshine
Despite the constant setbacks and drama we face day in and day out
It’s a challenge for a man to be a man we are tested everyday
In every way we are looked down upon we are to blame for some of this
We bring a lot of negativity on ourselves and we are faced with obstacles so sever
That it sometimes drives us to kill...but somehow we rise like the sunshine
The system is not designed for us so we work around the system
And to your surprise we rise like the sunshine

"Coulda Been Shoulda Been"

I lost many coulda been's shoulda been's
My heart spills blood and it's made of the opposite of lust
I meant well but it goes wrong I goes on
Off to the next coulda been shoulda been
I know it's the end because it's silent nights
U cannot predict the outcome when u first
Meet that person we all seek that person
Only to set ourselves up for disaster possibly possibly not
I try to prevent such a thing from happening
And women often hate me for this
Not understanding my logic
They don't understand that they need to understand him
And to understand him is to understand where he comes from
I have very little understand when it comes to marriage and relationships
U see my parents were never married
So it's hard to relate to what you've never seen
I've never seen so much pain inside 1 man
And that 4-letter word is a strange word to me
And I sometimes ask myself whatever happen?

"Under the Sun"

Under the sun corruption of the minds take place
All over the place
Corruption is in our educational institutions
We need more than just discussions we need solutions
Under the sun we have corruption in the work place
Even the bosses are scheming seemingly following the rules
But if you look closely you can see the masquerade
Under the shining sun darkness falls upon us and racism rips through the heart of the country
And under the sun more babies continue to give birth to babies
It's amazing how far we have come
But haven't gotten far enough ahead
Our kids are starving in bed and hip-hop and TV are the new teachers
Rap lords have replaced preachers
As a people we are not equal
Although they want us to believe so
Under the sun the seeds grow into young brothers who carry pis-tols
Weapons are a necessity where they are from
And kids from the ghetto can't catch a break
Under the sun the tragedies are unexplainable
But still we operate the best way we know how under the sun
Diseases are at an all time high under the sun nothing is pure
For some no cure under the sun
The foundation at home is broken hoping it gets better when sometimes it never does
You can't correct what never was
Under the sun

“Vis-‘A-Vis” (Vee-Za-Vee)

It’s far away right now hard for me to see hard for me to talk too
Days pass and I’m looking at time I would pay to spend it and go broke trying
It’s just a matter of it, the measures I would take would be extreme its sort of like a dream I mean I can feel it can you? My visions are filled with beautiful collisions
Between two faces gorgeous can’t help but to think how our seeds would be
Illuminate my world could be yours better yet I’ll share it with you is where I want to be for many days walks along the ocean with my hourglass goddess sincere when I speak this because she is, I’m only a few words away and for a second I thought I lost you but the sound of your heartbeat echoed through my
Eardrums and I followed the rhythm and found you my waterfall heaven rain drops touch and shower you , your smile put 1 on my face every time your skin tone so soft and smooth it changes my mood we connect like stars by the moon
Would you agree? I want to toast a glass of wine with you with your hair down and crown you queen of my world and I would drown in your elegant presence only for you to save me but if it was up to me I would stay there, I wish to make you happy and shine light on your existence as we enter each other’s dimensions
Did I forget to mention you’re beautiful and that your sexy eyes hypnotize mine?
Your lips crazy wet and keep me in check and your brain so intelligent for you I have the utmost respect play you never that, you know I like the smell of your neck, are you my mate and 1 is our soul we will soon see when we are vis-à-vis

"I Have To Laugh To Stop From Crying Sometimes"

I have to laugh to stop from crying sometimes
The harder I laugh the harder the more agony I feel
I smile with a frown on the inside but
You won't see it because I hide it behind the smile
I walk around as if nothing is wrong when everything is, you can't tell
But I have to laugh to stop from crying sometimes the pleasant expression on
My face is only skin deep and it is not true I'm surprised you don't see through
I guess you couldn't because I'm laughing
All the while on the interior a war is taking place taking up space in my conscience constantly fighting my demons
The reason I have this poker face
If you turn me inside out you will see that depression and stress live there
And they have for years now
They are not hard to be found
Breaking me down fast

Somehow I still manage to flash... a smile
Because I have to laugh to stop from crying sometimes

"Innocent Young Boy"

How can he go from an innocent young boy to a man with a I don't give a fuck
Attitude when you look at the baby pictures you don't know how he is going to turn out and before you know it the streets have turned him out
Some kids didn't grew up that way and are easily influenced some really don't have a choice nor a voice to express their opinion
Innocent young boy
Doing only what he sees he's hungry so he feeds off his environment becoming
The very thing he witness's because when he becomes a man he says
"Man that's all I know"
What he doesn't know is that there is more he could know and that he could turn into something remarkable
Innocent young boy not knowing his potential unlimited unstoppable
Only if he knew

“The Night Is Young”

2 early 2 tell never 2 early 2 see despair
As we know that it lurks
Behind what feels good for the moment 1 moment please
Here comes the 4-letter word again creeping without warning
Without hesitation but do I hesitate no!
Only when I don’t think that she is not interested
My sight blinded again as If I was born that way
I swore this would never happen again the 1st time the night was young
And it was 2 early 2 tell, I can’t go with my gut instinct because she put a
Funny feeling in my stomach and had it on lock that formed some type of
Circle in there and put it in a knot
And as soon as that happen I could see a future with her
But it’s 2 early 2 tell right now and the night is young

"Life Will Throw U A Curve"

As soon as you think everything is going good
Life will throw u a curve obstacles are set up to throw u off track
And to set u back a positive attitude is hard to maintain
I try to keep going regardless, regardless of what happens
Usually what happens is that life will throw u a curve
And set u up for disappointment
It's like u can't control the negative things that's going to happen to u

So what do I do?

“For The Moment with a Slight Chance of Forever”

Whatever hurt I caused put our bond on pause for the moment
With a slight chance of forever apologize I just because
I don’t know why, why am I
Could not tell you why
You asked and because of it you no longer speak a word in my direction
Did my imperfection cause this?
If so prepare yourself to feel this pain as long as you deal with him
Because he is not perfect

“The Eyes of Tomorrow”

I’m a child of God I got wings
Like a bird that’s trapped in a cage I want to be free
From all the evils among us
Not enough wives it’s too many baby mamas
You settling knowing you better than …that
We survived the worst crime in history
400 something years a thousand tears man I cried out both eyes and cried
Out for help I felt like the world was deaf it’s no love I shows none we frozen
In time my time will come in due time history proves we were born from the
Blood of kings and queens so it’s only right that we be who we truly are
Who I truly am I look into the eyes of tomorrow and see an uncertain future
Is what I see from a distance never the less with great persistence he pursues
Success which he’s been after since his 1st breath since his 1st step
A long way to go a long time coming this shapes the lives of those who are ambitious God granted wishes the sky is truly the limit and I’m a child of God
That has wings like a bird that’s trapped in a cage I want to be free

"U Know What I'm Saying"

Sometimes I'm amongst the clouds sometimes way over your head
Go head fa sho I know it's on what's going on ain't nothing same old folks frontin and stunt'n what's the deal I'm chillin well what's the word? It's all good but they still trippin tho Foreal? I ain't lying u buggin stop playing man she off the chain who u telling it's cool we cool I'll tell u what I grew up with him and that's my dog and if he don't get no bigger that's still my... fa sho it's on What's going on we balling they hatin quit hatin why u hatin they don't wanna see nobody get out the hood man that's crazy but that outfit is hot and I got on smell goods that's gonna kill'em u feel me? His jump shot was money and it still is he got handles 2 I'm just trying to handle life I know that's right show u right ...jack give me some dap on that peep dis peep game but look u got me? I got u let me holla at u man u ain't said nothing she got salty when she seen me with homegirl talking bout he tried to play me but she played herself as usual then she gone say to me oh u on that? Yeah I'm on that and yeah I talk slang that's a part of my thang u know what I'm saying?

“Misunderstood”

Misunderstood not understood at all
Was not born to fall it’s impossible you all get the wrong perception of him
Maybe it’s his fault because he uses discretion and you never see all the different
Sides of who he is he just is they say never judge a book by its cover you might only see the outside not knowing what lies beneath
They lye asleep misunderstanding that man and his intentions he shares a few laughs with you and in turn you think you know him assuming things that are most likely not true he is not you don’t get him misconstrued but the person he really is you will never understand

"Rain Drops Hit the Window Pain"

Rain drops hit the window pain
Snow hits the ground you can hear the sound of pain
As the water begins to thump harder when it makes
contact with the glass
It's hard to forget the abundance of rain which makes
you remember the amount of pain forever stained in my
memory killing me every time I'm reminded of that pain
the thought alone sticks like a knife in the back from a
fake friend invisible to those who have never experienced
this
I was born out of love and pain and these words soak in
the minds of those who relate like bodies in hot tubes
sometimes you can see the anger pour through my pores
the rain pours tremendously continuously more than
before he controls that anger comes when rain drops hit
the window pain

"So Be It"

So be it whatever happens happens
It don't matter anymore dreams are shattered in a matter of seconds
I'm done questioning everything I could care less less stress on me
Stay away from me I don't care if you understand or not so be it
My selfish ways are resurfacing
Resorting to what I know best
The rest is left up to I
So be it

“Breathe Out”

Take a deep breath
Now breathe out
Release any stress, anger or any negative thoughts you have
Control your breathing like you are in control of your own life
So take control of your life and breathe

Rest in peace Mary Alice Johnson
Rest in peace Edward James Johnson
Rest in peace Bertha Smith
Rest in peace Henry Smith
Rest in peace Great Grandpa Thomas Jones Sr
Rest in peace Karen Sims
Rest in peace Craig “Fly” Williams
Rest in peace Herbert Muhammad
Rest in peace Charles “Bumper” Herndon
Rest in peace Doug Johnson

1Love

Meet the Author

Varquis, a Gemini was born in Middletown Ohio. He graduated from Middletown High School where he excelled in English and was also a three year varsity basketball player. He spent a short stint at Moberly Junior College in Moberly Missouri.
He has written poetry since 1997-98 and also is a hip-hop recording artist and has written hip-hop songs since 1992. He wrote his first rap at the age of 8 years old. He released his first project as a apart of the hip-hop group State of the Art in 1997, he went on to release his first mixtape with his brother Dris titled Mixtape Vol.1 "Just The Beginning" in 2001.
In 2002 he released with partner/manager Damien McPherson "On Our Behalf", In 2005 Varquis along with his brother formed their independent company 1Life Entertainment Group LLC ,now officially known as the hip-hop group 1Life spawned Mixtape Vol2."Life As We Know It" which garnered great local success. In 2008 they released Mixtape 2.5 "The Prelude", also in 2010 he release an album as part of the hip-hop collective Truth Kamp titled "Tru-izm". Varquis is a self taught writer who inspires to obtain a publishing deal for his books of poetry and a distribution deal for his music. Varquis has several projects in the works which include: 1Life's "The Ink Pen Perspective", Varquis' solo projects 2 EPs and also a new book of poems "Untitled"
You can email him at Varquis@gmail.com or Google as well...Varquis.

1Life 1Love

www.ingramcontent.com/pod-product-compliance
Ingram Content Group UK Ltd.
Pitfield, Milton Keynes, MK11 3LW, UK
UKHW041902190726
13854UKWH00003B/1051